Need to Know
Meningitis

Kristina Routh

Heinemann
LIBRARY

www.heinemann.co.uk/library
Visit our website to find out more information about **Heinemann Library** books.

To order:
 Phone 44 (0) 1865 888066
 Send a fax to 44 (0) 1865 314091
 Visit the Heinemann Bookshop at www.heinemann.co.uk/library to browse our catalogue and order online.

Produced by Monkey Puzzle Media Ltd
Gissing's Farm, Fressingfield, Suffolk IP21 5SH, UK

First published in Great Britain by Heinemann Library, Halley Court, Jordan Hill, Oxford OX2 8EJ, part of Harcourt Education.
Heinemann is a registered trademark of Harcourt Education Ltd.

© Harcourt Education Ltd 2004
The moral right of the proprietor has been asserted.

Editorial: Cath Senker
Design: Jane Hawkins
Picture Research: Sally Cole
Consultant: Beverley Corbett, Educational and Training Manager, Meningitis Trust
Production: Viv Hichens

Originated by Ambassador Litho Ltd
Printed and bound in Hong Kong, China by South China Printing Company

ISBN 0 431 18844 0
08 07 06 05 04
10 9 8 7 6 5 4 3 2 1

British Library Cataloguing in Publication Data
Routh, Kristina
Meningitis. – (Need to know)
1.Meningitis – Juvenile literature
I.Title
616.8'2

Acknowledgements
The publishers would like to thank the following for permission to reproduce photographs: Alamy pp. 4 (Robert Harding Picture Library), 27 (Penny Tweedie), 37 top (Phototake Inc./Yoav Levy), 51 (David Young-Wolff); Corbis pp. 10 (Reflections/Jenny Woodcock), 11 (Bob Krist); Hulton Archive p. 7 (Fred Ramage); Imaging Body p. 20; Meningitis Trust pp. 14, 17, 41; Panos Pictures p. 26 (Betty Press); PA Photos pp. 29 (EPA), 37 bottom (Owen Humphreys), 46 (David Kendal); Science Photo Library pp. 1 (James Prince), 8 (Simon Fraser/Royal Victoria Infimary, Newcastle-upon-Tyne), 15 (Gary Parker), 16 (Dr Kari Lounatmaa), 19 (James Prince), 22 (Dr P Marazzi), 30 (John Cole), 32 (Simon Fraser/Royal Victoria Infirmary, Newcastle-upon-Tyne), 33 (TEK Image), 34 (Larry Mulvehill), 40 (Mauro Fermariello), 43 (Adam Hart-Davis), 49 (Mike Miller); Topham Picturepoint pp. 13 (Image Works), 23 (Image Works/Bob Daemmrich), 24 (Image Works/Larry Kolvoord), 28 (Image Works/Bob Daemmrich), 39 (Image Works/Ellen Senisi), 44 (Photri); Wellcome Library, London p. 6.

Cover photographs reproduced with permission of SPL (James Prince) and SPL (Dr Kari Lounatmaa).

The author and publishers would like to thank the Meningitis Research Foundation, UK for their help in the preparation of this book and for providing the case study on page 12; the Meningitis Centre, Australia for the case study on page 19; the Meningitis Foundation of America for information for the case studies on page 23 and pages 40–41, and Kelly and her family for the case study on pages 40–41. We would like to thank the Meningitis Trust, UK for providing photos and checking the text.

Every effort has been made to contact copyright holders of any material reproduced in this book. Any omissions will be rectified in subsequent printings if notice is given to the publishers.

Some names in this text have been changed to protect the privacy of the individuals quoted.

Contents

Any words appearing in the text in bold, **like this**, are explained in the Glossary.

Introducing meningitis

Meningitis occurs all over the world; it is truly a global disease. Most people have read newspaper stories about meningitis or seen programmes on television about it. Meningitis is often spoken about as a 'killer' disease, and one that can strike unexpectedly, especially in babies and children.

As is often the case, the real facts are more complicated. It is true that meningitis can kill, but in most cases those who suffer from it recover. The disease can leave a person with serious and disabling after-effects, such as deafness or **epilepsy**. Yet in most cases this does not happen.

A severe headache is one of the most common symptoms of meningitis.

Meningitis is much more common in babies and children but it can also affect healthy teenagers and adults. People who have a weak **immune system**, perhaps because of disease or old age, are also at risk.

So what is meningitis?

Meningitis is a serious infection that affects the delicate **membranes** covering the brain and **spinal cord**. Among other things, it may cause headaches, vomiting, fever and mental confusion. In the most severe cases of the disease, the individual becomes so ill that he or she must be taken to hospital immediately to receive life-saving treatment.

There are lots of different **micro-organisms** that can cause meningitis. Most cases are caused by **viruses** or a few particular types of **bacteria**. Although viral meningitis can sometimes be quite serious, it is the bacterial form of the disease that is most likely to cause severe problems.

Bacterial meningitis is particularly likely to be harmful when it is accompanied by **septicaemia** – infection of the blood (see page 14).

Education

In many cases, the danger with meningitis comes when it is not recognized early enough. People have died who might have been saved if only they had been given treatment sooner. Health departments and charitable meningitis organizations work hard to publicize the signs and symptoms of meningitis so that people will know when to seek medical help urgently. These organizations also provide information for the media so that the reporting of cases of meningitis can be more balanced and informative, and less alarming.

"Meningitis and septicaemia are life-threatening diseases. Knowing the signs and symptoms of meningitis and septicaemia, and acting quickly to get medical help, can save lives."

(The Meningitis Research Foundation, UK)

Meningitis over the years

One of the most important types of meningitis – **meningococcal meningitis** (see page 16) – was first described in 1805 by Gaspard Vieusseux, a doctor in Geneva, Switzerland. Unlike some other infectious diseases – such as **tuberculosis**, which had been documented for thousands of years – there was very little description of meningitis before the beginning of the 19th century.

Epidemics

From the beginning of that century, **epidemics** (large **outbreaks**) of meningococcal meningitis began to occur. From 1806 to 1816 there were many cases in the USA, especially in New England. The first book about meningococcal meningitis – or 'spotted fever' as it was known – was written by Elisha North of Connecticut, USA and was published in 1811.

As the 19th century progressed, the disease began to appear in many different countries. Europe was badly affected, with many deaths being caused in countries such as France, Italy and Germany. Between 1854 and 1861, 4100 people died in Sweden alone and many more were left in poor health. By 1875, reports of meningococcal meningitis had started to come from Africa, Asia and Australia. The **bacteria** that cause this type of meningitis – *Neisseria meningitidis* (or meningococci) – were identified in 1887 by Anton Weichselbaum of Vienna, Austria.

The scientist, Anton Weichselbaum.

Epidemics of meningococcal meningitis have been particularly associated with times of war, when there are large-scale movements of people and many have to live crowded together in poor conditions. The disease was rife during the time of the American Civil War (1861–65) and there were epidemics during both the First and Second World Wars (1914–18 and 1939–45).

Treatment

Before **antibiotics** were introduced around 70 years ago, there was little that could be done to treat meningitis. Over three-quarters of all people who got meningococcal meningitis died, and many more were left disabled.

In the late 1930s, the first antibiotics were used against meningitis. Sulfanilamide was given to soldiers in the French Foreign Legion serving in West Africa during an outbreak of the disease. While stocks lasted, the death rate was reduced from 75 per cent to 11 per cent.

Penicillin, which first became widely used in the 1940s, proved very effective against meningitis. At last, doctors had a reliable way to combat this terrible disease. And today, in the 21st century, penicillin remains one of the most important antibiotics for treating bacterial meningitis.

The many causes of meningitis

Meningitis is the infection of the **meninges**, the delicate **membranes** that cover and protect the brain and **spinal cord**. There are three layers of membranes: the dura is the tough outer layer. The arachnoid is the middle layer (named for its spider-like appearance) and the pia is the inner layer, which is rich in blood vessels. The brain and spinal cord are bathed in a special liquid called **cerebrospinal fluid** (CSF). This also becomes infected in meningitis.

Once an infection has taken hold in the meninges, it can be hard for the body to fight it. There are not many defence cells or **antibodies** in the CSF like there are in the blood. When the body does fight back, it causes **inflammation**, which may then damage the brain.

brain

This brain scan shows someone with meningitis. The areas highlighted in yellow are patches of inflammation caused by the infection.

spinal cord

Viruses

There are many different kinds of organism that can cause meningitis. The most common are **viruses**. Viruses are incredibly tiny **micro-organisms**, much too small to be seen under a normal microscope. They are so small that they can even infect **bacteria**! Viral meningitis is usually less serious than bacterial meningitis – which is lucky, because there are no medicines to treat it. Most people with viral meningitis get better after a few weeks.

Types of bacterial meningitis:

- **Pneumococcal meningitis**, caused by the bacterium *Streptococcus pneumoniae*.
- **Meningococcal meningitis**, caused by the bacterium *Neisseria meningitidis*.
- **Hib meningitis**, caused by the bacterium *Haemophilus influenzae*, type b.

Bacteria

Bacteria are small organisms that can be seen in the laboratory under a microscope. Taken as a group, they are the second most common cause of meningitis. Bacterial meningitis tends to be more serious than viral meningitis, and may even cause death. There may be an associated infection of the bloodstream, known as **septicaemia**, which is usually serious. However, unlike viruses, bacteria can be killed by medicines – **antibiotics** – and so treatment is available.

Meningitis can also be caused by some other bacteria, including *Escherichia coli* (*E. coli*), Group B streptococci, salmonella and *Mycobacterium tuberculosis*, the bacteria responsible for **tuberculosis** (see page 24).

Other causes

Although meningitis is usually caused by viruses or bacteria, there are some rare cases where the disease is caused by certain types of **fungi** or **protozoa** (see page 25).

How does meningitis spread?

How meningitis spreads depends upon whether **viruses** or **bacteria** are causing the disease.

Viral meningitis

Viral meningitis can occur in **outbreaks**, sometimes at particular times of the year. The viruses that are most likely to cause meningitis can be spread in two main ways:

- Respiratory droplets – tiny drops of saliva or mucus from the nose, which are coughed, sneezed or even breathed out. These can be breathed in by someone else, or may be passed on when shaking hands with an infected person.

- Via faeces. The viruses may live in the intestines and get on to the hands after an infected person uses the toilet or changes a baby's nappy. If the person does not wash his or her hands properly, the virus may be passed on to another person. This can happen by touching food that someone else will eat. Young children, who may not remember to wash their hands, often pass on viruses in this way.

Outbreaks of bacterial meningitis can occur in military camps, where people live close together.

Bacterial meningitis

The bacteria that can cause bacterial meningitis often live quite harmlessly for weeks or months in the lining of the nose and throat of healthy people. This is known as **colonization**. At any one time, between 10 and 25 per cent of people are colonized in this way.

Occasionally, these bacteria get past the body's defences to enter the bloodstream. Then they may cause **septicaemia** or travel to the **meninges** to cause meningitis – or sometimes both.

Of the types of bacterial meningitis, only **meningococcal meningitis** occurs in outbreaks. **Pneumococcal meningitis** and **Hib meningitis** do not seem to spread from person to person.

Meningococcal bacteria are fragile and die quite quickly outside the body. This means that they can only be passed from person to person through close contact. Kissing is a well-known way of passing on these bacteria. Just being near to an infected person when he or she sneezes or coughs can cause infection too. This kind of meningitis usually only spreads within a community where people spend a lot of time close together. For example, there have been outbreaks in schools and military training camps.

Symptoms of meningitis

Recognizing meningitis is crucial. In some cases, early treatment may mean the difference between life and death. At first, the symptoms might not be clear, or may seem like those of flu. But in meningitis, the infected person can become very ill. Symptoms of viral meningitis may be similar to those of bacterial meningitis, but are usually not so severe.

Typical symptoms

These symptoms may not appear in any particular order, and some may not appear at all. The illness may develop over several days or sometimes in a few hours. The best-known symptoms of meningitis, and meningococcal **septicaemia**, include:

- a headache, which is usually severe
- neck stiffness, which may mean the sufferer is unable to touch his or her chin to the chest
- **photophobia** – an intense dislike of bright light
- drowsiness or confusion; there may even be seizures
- fever: there may be a high temperature, perhaps with cold hands and feet

- vomiting, sometimes even diarrhoea
- a rash, where there is septicaemia (see page 14)
- joint pain or aching, especially in septicaemia.

Sally's story

Sally was fifteen when she developed **meningococcal meningitis** and septicaemia. She recalls, 'I couldn't stop vomiting – I thought I had eaten something that had made me ill. I tried to go upstairs but I couldn't get past the first step. My father later said that I was drifting in and out of consciousness. I was so bad that he had to help me get undressed and get into bed. I had a very high temperature, so he tried giving me sponge baths to keep it down. When the doctor came to my house, she immediately noticed two 'bruises' on my upper arm that had just started to appear. She diagnosed **meningococcal disease** straight away and called an ambulance. I was taken to hospital, the ambulance siren blaring all the way.'

Babies and young children

Many cases of meningitis are in babies and young children, who often do not show the typical symptoms. Parents who are worried that their baby might have meningitis should look out for:

- a high-pitched, moaning cry
- fever, perhaps with cold hands and feet
- vomiting
- refusing feeds
- floppiness when being picked up
- pale, blotchy skin
- difficulty in waking the child
- a rash, where there is septicaemia.

Meningitis and meningococcal septicaemia require urgent medical attention. Anyone who is in any doubt should see a doctor.

A raised temperature is one of the common signs of meningitis.

Types of meningitis

Blood poisoning

Septicaemia is a bacterial infection of the blood, also known as blood poisoning. It is usually a serious and life-threatening condition. Septicaemia is included here because the **bacteria** that cause meningitis may also cause septicaemia, sometimes together with meningitis, sometimes alone.

Septicaemia is especially likely to occur with infection by meningococci. When someone has both **meningococcal meningitis** and septicaemia, it is commonly called **meningococcal disease**. It is not known why some people develop meningitis, some develop septicaemia, and some develop both.

What happens?

In septicaemia, bacteria multiply rapidly within the bloodstream and produce poisons that damage the walls of the blood vessels. Blood can then leak out of the blood vessels into the surrounding **tissues**. This leakage of blood leads to the major symptoms of septicaemia:

- A rash. Blood leaking out into the tissues under the skin causes the distinctive rash that often appears in meningococcal disease (see glass tumbler test below and opposite). The rash starts as tiny red spots but these soon get larger and turn into purple 'bruises'.
- Raised heart rate. As more and more blood is lost from the bloodstream into the tissues, the heart pumps faster in an attempt to increase the circulation.
- Cold hands and feet. The circulatory system starts to 'shut down', keeping what blood there is for the vital internal organs rather than for the limbs.

This rash has not faded under the glass. It might be due to meningococcal septicaemia.

- Multiple organ failure. Eventually, the lack of blood for the vital internal organs causes them to fail and death often follows.

Meningococcal septicaemia is a medical emergency. Most deaths from meningococcal disease are due to the septicaemia. Only prompt treatment with **antibiotics** gives an infected person a good chance of survival.

Intravenous antibiotics are needed if someone has bacterial meningitis.

The glass tumbler test

The glass tumbler test is a simple way to tell if a skin rash could be due to meningococcal septicaemia. The meningococcal rash is said to be non-blanching, which means that it does not fade (blanch, or whiten) if pressure is applied to it. Other less harmful rashes will blanch if pressed.

A glass tumbler (or any piece of safe, clear glass) is pressed firmly against the rash. The rash is then looked at through the glass to see if it has whitened, or disappeared. If it is still present, then it might be due to meningococcal septicaemia. Medical attention should be sought straight away.

Meningococcal meningitis

The most common type of bacteria to cause meningitis is known as *Neisseria meningitidis* (or meningococci). These bacteria are found in people all around the world. Up to one quarter of individuals carry them harmlessly in their throats. It is only occasionally that they go on to cause infection, although **epidemics** can occur, affecting many people. Meningococci can cause both meningitis and septicaemia.

In many countries, such as the USA, UK and Australia, cases of meningococcal meningitis tend to occur seasonally in the winter and early spring. For some reason, the disease seems to appear in ten to fifteen year cycles, although it never goes away completely.

Meningococcal meningitis and septicaemia can affect people of all ages but is most common in young children and teenagers. Around

The bacteria that cause meningococcal meningitis, *Neisseria meningitidis*, greatly magnified by a powerful electron microscope.

5 to 10 per cent of people who get meningococcal disease will die, usually due to septicaemia. Many people recover completely but some are left with severe and disabling after-effects such as deafness, **epilepsy**, muscle weakness or even loss of limbs due to **amputations**.

A dangerous infection

Meningococcal disease can be treated with antibiotics, but even with modern medical treatment this can be a life-threatening infection. It is vital that treatment starts as early as possible.

Types of meningococcus

Like many bacteria, **meningococci** can be divided into several groups, or **serogroups**. The five groups that are responsible for most of the cases of meningococcal disease around the world today are known as B, C, A, Y and W-135.

The B and C groups are the most common types found in many **developed countries** such as the UK, USA, Australia and New Zealand. There is a **vaccine** for group C, but none yet for group B, which tends to be more common. Group Y occurs in the USA but is rare in Europe and Australasia.

Group A is common in **sub-Saharan Africa** (where it causes large epidemics), Pakistan, Nepal and parts of India. W-135 has only recently emerged as an important group. Most of the cases are in Africa but this group is now spreading to other regions.

Doctors may recommend websites to people wanting to find out more about meningitis.

Types of meningitis

Pneumococcal meningitis

Pneumococcal meningitis is caused by bacteria called *Streptococcus pneumoniae* (or pneumococci), which many people carry harmlessly in the back of the nose and throat. They can cause ear and sinus infections, **pneumonia**, meningitis and septicaemia.

Pneumococci are the second most common cause of meningitis in the USA and UK. This type of meningitis is not contagious (catching) and does not occur in **outbreaks**. The symptoms tend to be the same as for other types of meningitis but there is no rash.

Pneumococcal meningitis has a higher fatality rate and risk of serious after-effects, such as deafness and brain damage, than meningococcal disease. In many countries, a vaccine is available for those at greatest risk.

(Opposite) Pneumococcal meningitis is a serious disease, often requiring intensive care in hospital.

Who gets this disease?

Most cases of pneumococcal meningitis are seen in young children and the elderly. People with a medical condition that lowers their immunity also have a higher risk. They include those who:

- do not have a **spleen** because it has been injured or removed, or have a poorly functioning spleen, such as in **sickle cell disorder**. (The spleen forms part of the body's **immune system**.)
- have a long-standing disease of the heart, lung, kidney or liver
- have diabetes
- have a head injury or defect in their skull through which the bacteria can spread
- have low immunity because of **HIV infection** or because they are taking medicines that affect their immune system (for cancer, or after an organ transplant)
- have cochlear implants – these are mechanical devices implanted in the inner ear to aid hearing. They may allow bacteria to reach the **meninges** from the ear.

Aimee's story

Aimee had always been a happy, healthy baby so her parents were quite worried when she suddenly seemed unwell. Aimee's sister Jackie remembers, 'She was restless, whingeing and had a high temperature that wouldn't come down.' After several trips to the family doctor, Aimee was rushed to hospital.

Tests showed that Aimee had pneumococcal meningitis. She spent the next two weeks fighting for her life while the doctors and nurses did all they could to treat her. 'Everyone in my family and the doctors were unsure whether or not Aimee was going to make it,' says Jackie. But Aimee fought hard and survived. She has been left with many medical problems, including epilepsy and deafness, but Jackie proudly says, 'Even with all these disabilities, today she is a happy, healthy young lady.'

Types of meningitis

Hib meningitis

Hib stands for '*Haemophilus influenzae*, capsulated Pittman type b', a very long name for a very small bacterium! **Hib meningitis** used to be the most common type of meningitis in children under five in the USA, UK, Australia and New Zealand. Thanks to the introduction of a vaccine in the early 1990s, it has become extremely rare in these countries.

Routine infant immunizations have meant that Hib meningitis is now rare in many countries.

The Hib vaccine is now part of the routine vaccination schedule for young babies in many developed countries. However, in countries that do not use it, this type of meningitis is still common among young children.

Hib infections

Hib may be carried harmlessly in the back of the throat or may cause mild infections of the ear or respiratory tract (windpipe and lungs). Occasionally, the bacteria cause serious infections, including epiglottitis (**inflammation** of the epiglottis, the flap at the top of the windpipe), septicaemia, cellulitis (infection of the tissues) and joint infections. They can also cause meningitis.

Hib meningitis has the same symptoms as the other forms of bacterial meningitis, although there is not usually a rash. Over 95 per cent of children with Hib meningitis survive. In most cases, there is a full recovery, but after-effects such as deafness, brain damage and epilepsy still occur in around 12 per cent of sufferers.

Who gets Hib?

Nearly all those who are affected by Hib meningitis are young children between the ages of three months and five years. The disease is unusual outside this age range and is very rare indeed among adults.

This is probably because between three months and five years the child does not have enough **antibodies** – special defence chemicals – to fight off Hib infection. Before it is three months old, the baby still has some protective antibodies received from the mother while in the womb. After birth, these gradually decline and the baby has to start making its own antibodies. By the time the child is five years old, he or she has usually made enough antibodies to be able to fight off attacks from the Hib bacteria.

If a person's immune system becomes weak, perhaps because of long-standing disease, then he or she may be again at a higher risk of getting Hib, even as an adult.

Types of meningitis

Viral meningitis

Viral meningitis is probably more common than bacterial meningitis but it is generally less serious. It tends to affect children more than adults. The symptoms are usually mild. The person may feel generally unwell, perhaps with a headache and a raised temperature. Sometimes, the symptoms are more severe, like those of bacterial meningitis. There is usually no rash.

Antibiotics do not kill **viruses**, so there are no medicines that can be given to treat this kind of meningitis. Fortunately, most people get better with simple treatments, such as painkillers for headaches and anti-sickness medicines for vomiting.

People with viral meningitis do not usually suffer the severe after-effects that may happen with bacterial meningitis. And viral meningitis is rarely fatal.

Which viruses cause it?

Many different viruses can cause meningitis but most cases are caused by just a few, including:

- enteroviruses – these cause most cases of viral meningitis. There are about 80 different types, most belonging to the two groups Coxsackie viruses and echoviruses. These usually cause only mild illness.
- mumps and measles. The mumps virus in particular used to be a common cause of meningitis in children. Now that most children receive the MMR (Measles, Mumps and Rubella) vaccine, this type of meningitis is rare in developed countries.
- herpes viruses. These viruses, which can cause cold sores around the mouth, sometimes lead to a mild form of meningitis.

In most cases, doctors never find out which virus is causing the illness.

The herpes virus that causes cold sores around the mouth can sometimes also cause meningitis.

Katie's story

Katie, a 30-year-old woman from the USA, had a particularly nasty time with viral meningitis. It came on gradually over four weeks. She remembers, 'All I could do was lie in agony as my head felt like it was held in a vice. It came to the point where eating was no longer enjoyable because the nausea [sickness] was so awful. I was sick two or three times every day.' Katie was eventually diagnosed with severe viral meningitis and spent some time in hospital. After coming home it took her another four months to feel back to normal. She says, 'I did get better but it was a long and frustrating road with good days and bad days.'

Most people with viral meningitis simply need to rest until they feel better.

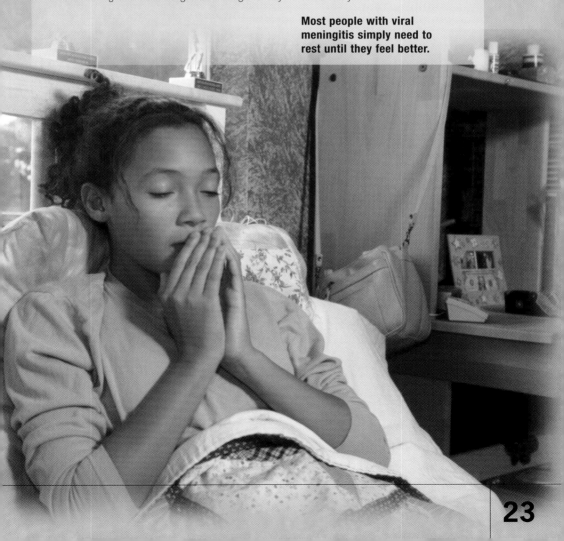

Rare forms of meningitis

Most cases of meningitis are caused by **viruses** or by the three **bacteria** named previously. However, there are many other tiny **micro-organisms** that can sometimes cause meningitis.

Tuberculosis

The bacteria that cause **tuberculosis** (TB), *Mycobacterium tuberculosis*, can occasionally cause a severe and often fatal form of meningitis. Children are particularly at risk in areas of the world where there is a lot of TB. In most **developed countries**, tuberculosis is relatively less common. TB meningitis usually affects the elderly, those with weak **immune systems** because of other illness, and immigrants who were born in countries with high rates of TB.

Fungi

Fungal meningitis is rare, with nearly all cases being in people whose immune systems are weaker than normal. Most at risk today are those who have **HIV**/AIDS.

Cryptococcus neoformans, the type of **fungus** that is most likely to cause meningitis, normally lives harmlessly in the environment and is found throughout the world. One of the main ways that humans become infected is by inhaling particles from dried bird droppings.

Protozoa

Protozoa are single-celled creatures that are considered to be tiny animals. One type, *Naegleria fowleri*, is a well-known cause of meningitis. It lives in freshwater lakes and swimming pools in very warm areas of the world, including the southern states of the USA and some parts of Australia. People can become infected after swimming or playing in the water. The organism goes up into the nose and from there makes it way to the brain, causing a serious (and often fatal) form of meningitis. Luckily, this is an extremely rare infection!

Reptiles and salmonella

Salmonella is a type of bacteria that is best known for causing food poisoning. It can occasionally cause meningitis, usually in babies and young children.

One unusual source of infection with salmonella is a pet reptile. Reptiles, such as snakes, iguanas and turtles, often carry salmonella bacteria in their intestines. These may then be passed on to people while handling the animal. There have been many cases of children becoming ill after playing with reptiles. On the occasions that meningitis has developed, some have even died. Washing hands after playing with pets is a simple and effective way of preventing the spread of infection in this way.

The tiny organism *Naegleria fowleri* may lurk in this lake.

Who is affected by meningitis?

Meningitis is not a common disease, but it can have such serious consequences that it is certainly an important one to know about.

Viral meningitis

It is hard to know how common viral meningitis is. In many cases, people who get it are not unwell enough to seek medical attention. It probably occurs more frequently than the bacterial forms.

Viral meningitis is more common in **developing countries**, where there may be a lack of good **sanitation** and clean water for washing. This makes it easier for **viruses** to spread from person to person.

Meningitis is common in places where there is poor sanitation.

Meningococcal meningitis

Meningococcal disease is said to be endemic – present at all times – throughout the world.

- The USA, with a population of 280 million, has about 3000 cases a year. Since 1991, cases among young people aged 15–24 have almost doubled.
- The UK, with a population of nearly 60 million, has about 2500 cases each year.
- Australia, with a population of over 19 million, has about 650 cases a year.
- New Zealand, with a population of nearly 4 million, is currently in the grip of a long **meningococcal meningitis epidemic**, with around 650 cases a year.

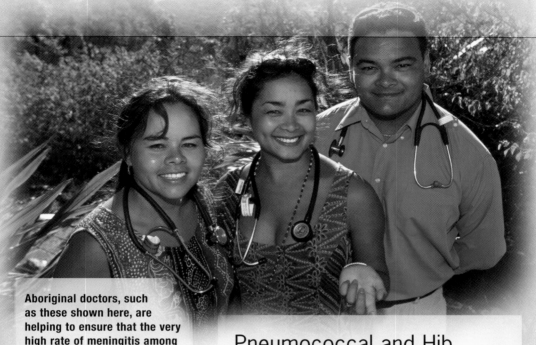

Aboriginal doctors, such as these shown here, are helping to ensure that the very high rate of meningitis among Aboriginal Australians is taken seriously.

ffWe are currently in the eleventh year of an epidemic that is expected to continue for a further ten years. There is no sign of the epidemic abating.**JJ**

(Dr Jane O'Hallahan, New Zealand Public Health Medicine Specialist, 2001)

Pneumococcal and Hib meningitis

Pneumococcal meningitis is the most common form of bacterial meningitis in adults. In many countries, such as the USA, UK, Australia and New Zealand, it is the second most common cause of meningitis in all ages. In the USA for instance, there are around 1400 cases per year. The highest rate of pneumococcal meningitis in the world – around 20 times the rate amongst non-Aboriginal Australians – is found among some Aboriginal communities in Australia.

In the countries that use the **vaccine**, **Hib meningitis** is now much less common than it was. For example, in the mid-1980s there were about 13,000 cases a year in the USA. Now there are only a few hundred.

Who is affected by meningitis?

Who is at risk?

Anyone can get meningitis, but it is more likely to affect some groups of people than others. Different types of meningitis tend to affect different groups of people but those most at risk are:

- babies, especially newborns, and young children
- teenagers and young people, from meningococcal disease
- the elderly, who are particularly likely to get pneumococcal meningitis
- those with a weak **immune system**, including people with **HIV**/AIDS, cancer, or chronic (long-term) disease. People in these groups are more likely than others to get the rarer forms of meningitis.

Schools and colleges

There have been many **outbreaks** of meningococcal meningitis in places where young people live or work closely together, such as in schools, universities and military training camps. In one case in Sydney, Australia, an outbreak was associated with a popular nightclub. Many colleges in the USA, UK, Australia and New Zealand provide information leaflets to the new intake of students every year. The leaflets explain the symptoms of meningitis and when medical help is urgently needed.

Outbreaks of meningitis can occur in places where young people live or work closely together, such as universities.

Meningitis epidemics

People in some countries, such as in the so-called 'meningitis belt' of **sub-Saharan Africa**, have a high risk of getting meningococcal meningitis. Here, meningococcal disease is epidemic. Every few years, there are large outbreaks that affect a significant proportion of the population in those areas. During an epidemic, as many as 2 per cent of people may be affected, which is 2000 people in every 100,000! Epidemics do also occur in **developed countries**, but much less frequently.

The Hajj and meningococcal disease

The Hajj is the annual Islamic pilgrimage to the holy cities of Makkah and Madinah in Saudi Arabia. Several million people from around the world take part, spending much of the time gathered together in large crowds. This allows **bacteria**, including meningococci, to spread easily.

There have been many cases of meningococcal disease among people who have returned home from the Hajj, and among their close contacts. In 2000, there was an international outbreak with 60 deaths, and in 2001, 10 people died in the UK alone. Many of these cases were caused by a relatively new **serogroup** of **meningococcus**, W-135 (see page 17).

Hajj pilgrims now have to be vaccinated against meningococcal disease, including W-135, before they can obtain a travel visa for Saudi Arabia.

This man is being immunized against meningitis before going on the Hajj.

Who is affected by meningitis?

Newborn babies

Newborn babies are a special case when it comes to meningitis. They are more likely to get it than older children because their immune systems are not so well developed. The bacteria involved are usually different from the three that affect older children and adults. Newborn babies are more likely to die than older children or to be left with serious after-effects.

Hundreds of different types of bacteria may cause meningitis in newborn babies. The two most common are Group B streptococci (sometimes known as GBS) and *Escherichia coli* (*E. coli*). These often live quite harmlessly in the intestinal tract (gut)

and vagina of the mother. They can be passed on to the baby during birth or from other people's hands after birth. It is very rare for these bacteria to cause meningitis in older children and adults.

Group B streptococci

Group B streptococci infections of newborns have become more common over the last 20 years. For every thousand babies that are born, between two and eight of them will get a GBS infection. GBS are the most common cause of meningitis and **septicaemia** in newborn babies in the USA, UK and Australia. Infection may start either just before or during birth (called early onset) or the illness may start a few weeks later (when it is called late onset infection).

Babies like this one, born 10 weeks early, have an increased risk of meningitis.

E. coli

Everyone carries *E. coli* in his or her intestines. These do not usually do any harm, but there are some uncommon strains that can cause disease. *E. coli* are passed to the baby from either the mother or other people who handle him or her. The *E. coli* can then invade the baby's bloodstream, causing septicaemia and meningitis.

Risk factors

Some newborn babies are more likely than others to suffer from meningitis:

- pre-term (early) babies, especially those that are born more than six or seven weeks early. The normal length of pregnancy – full term – is 40 weeks.
- low birth-weight babies. These are babies that weigh less than 2 kg at birth, and especially tiny ones, weighing less than 1 kg. Most full-term babies weigh between 2.5 and 4.25 kg at birth.
- those who had difficulties during birth. Sometimes the baby needs a lot of help to be born, or may go for a short time without enough oxygen.

Treating meningitis

Testing for meningitis

The diagnosis of meningitis is made with the help of the hospital **microbiology laboratory**. Two types of samples are taken – **cerebrospinal fluid** (CSF) and blood. A sample of CSF is collected during a **lumbar puncture**. This is carried out in hospital by trained medical staff (if the patient is well enough). The doctor inserts a fine needle into the area around the spine and draws out a small sample of fluid.

In bacterial meningitis, **bacteria** can usually be found circulating in the bloodstream. A sample of blood is taken from a vein, and is immediately put into bottles containing a special liquid full of nutrients to help the bacteria to grow.

In the laboratory

The samples are sent immediately to the microbiology laboratory to be examined. There are two main types of test, microscopy and culture. Most hospital laboratories have a microbiologist available 24 hours a day. He or she will look at the CSF sample straight away using a microscope, examining it for **white blood cells** and bacteria.

Normal CSF is clear, with no white blood cells. In meningitis, the CSF may look cloudy, and contain lots of white blood cells that the body is using to defend itself. The type of white blood cells is usually different for viral meningitis than for bacterial. Sometimes bacteria are seen in the CSF. In many cases, the microbiologist can tell which type of bacteria they are just by looking. **Viruses** are too small to be seen in this way.

Here, a cerebrospinal fluid sample is being collected by a doctor during a lumbar puncture.

Whether or not anything is seen, the microbiologist will try to grow bacteria from both the CSF and the blood samples. He or she spreads some of the samples on to agar plates (agar is a special hard jelly that contains nutrients for bacteria). The plates are placed in an incubator, a machine to keep them warm so the bacteria can grow.

Rapid tests

Sometimes bacteria do not appear on microscopy, or grow on agar jelly, even if the patient has bacterial meningitis. This may be because the patient had been given **antibiotics** before the samples were taken. Many laboratories now have a range of rapid tests that can determine whether bacteria, even dead ones, are present in CSF samples. These tests use specially designed **antibodies** that clump together when bacteria are present. Rapid tests are not yet completely reliable, but are improving all the time.

A microbiologist examines body cells grown on the base of a special bottle.

Treating meningitis

The first few hours

For some people, meningitis develops slowly, over a period of several days, but for many it comes on very suddenly. This is especially true in cases of meningococcal **septicaemia**, in which the blood is infected.

Symptoms can vary. Babies may become unwell very quickly, and it is often not clear what is making them upset. Older people are more likely to have the usual meningitis symptoms, which include headache, vomiting and fever.

Seeking medical help

Unless the symptoms of meningitis are very mild, most people will go to see their family doctor fairly quickly. It can be difficult to decide whether someone has meningitis, especially a young child, so admission to hospital for tests may be needed.

If there is a rash, **meningococcal disease** will be suspected. This is a medical emergency and family doctors usually keep supplies of suitable antibiotics just in case. These are injected immediately. Then the person is rushed straight to hospital.

In the hospital

After arriving in the hospital emergency department, the person with meningitis may need a lot of special care straight away. Fluids are given **intravenously** – into the vein through a drip – to replace any lost through vomiting. Painkillers may be given if headaches are severe, and anti-sickness medicine may be required. Above all, the patient needs antibiotics. These have to be given intravenously so that they can get to the infected areas around the brain as rapidly as possible. It is likely that the patient will remain in hospital for at least a few days if not longer.

Meningitis may be a medical emergency and the patient may have to be rushed to hospital.

Treating meningitis

Hospital care

Someone who has a severe case of meningitis or septicaemia may need special care in hospital for quite a long time – perhaps weeks or even months. Meningococcal disease in particular can make a person extremely ill. He or she may need to stay in the **Intensive Care Unit** (ICU).

The Intensive Care Unit

The ICU is a special ward where extremely sick people are cared for. There are many more doctors and nurses than there are on general wards. A lot of specialized equipment is used. People in intensive care often have several different tubes carrying fluids and medicines into their bodies. They are surrounded by various types of machines that monitor the body's functions, such as heart rate and breathing.

It can be distressing for the family to see their loved one in such a strange environment, especially if it is a child. Although it can be stressful for the patients themselves, many say they cannot remember much about it. This may be due to the medicines they have been given as well as the illness itself.

For someone with **meningococcal meningitis** and septicaemia, the time in the ICU may be spent fighting for their lives. Many will recover, some completely, others with medical problems that will be with them all their lives. Sadly, despite all the antibiotics, special equipment and dedicated medical and nursing care, some will die.

"The doctors let us touch his head and tell him how much we loved him. Our hearts were broken, we had lost our son, the laughter of our lives."

(John, from Maryland, USA, whose son Sam died from meningococcal disease aged 18, National Meningitis Association, USA)

This boy is being taught to use his prosthetic (false) arm after losing his limb to septicaemia.

Serious after-effects

Many people who are treated in hospital for meningitis recover fairly quickly and soon go home to continue their lives. However, meningitis can leave serious after-effects. Septicaemia can lead to stiffness of the joints, **arthritis**, scarring and skin damage. Kidney or lung damage may occur, and it may even become necessary for fingers, toes, arms or legs to be **amputated**.

Learning to walk again after losing limbs can take many months.

Living with the consequences

Some of the after-effects that are a consequence of meningitis can be quite serious. Complications can occur with any type of meningitis but are more common after bacterial meningitis. About one in ten people who have **meningococcal disease** are left with disabling after-effects. **Pneumococcal meningitis**, and meningitis in newborn babies, are even more likely to cause long-term problems. After-effects may include:

- memory loss and lack of concentration
- clumsiness
- headaches
- deafness, or hearing problems
- learning difficulties
- **epilepsy** (seizures)
- weakness or paralysis of part of the body
- speech problems
- eyesight difficulties.

If there are serious after-effects, there will be a longer period of rehabilitation, or getting back to normal. The individual will need extra help from healthcare staff to fully recover. For some, this means many months in hospital, which can cause real problems for family life, education or employment.

Emotional after-effects

For many people, it takes a long time to recover from the upsetting experience of having meningitis. This is especially true if the person had to be treated in hospital for a long time. Young children may become clingy, throw tantrums and may wet their beds at night. Teenagers might have problems later in completing their education, getting jobs, forming relationships and becoming independent adults. People who have had meningitis can find that their moods change suddenly, going from happy to sad for no apparent reason. Many people say that they have good days and bad days.

For some people the experience of being so ill even has some benefits. As Chelsea (see quotation opposite) says, 'I am changed for the better as I value life more, and realize my own mortality. I want to make things count.'

People who are recovering from meningitis may need extra support from their family and friends for a while. Teachers and employers need to be aware of what a difficult time it has been for the child or adult returning after meningitis.

"When the teacher is talking and writing on the board and we are expected to listen and write notes at the same time, I have problems. I can do one thing or the other, but not both."

(Chelsea, aged 16, after recovering from meningitis, The Meningitis Foundation of America)

Living with the consequences

Kelly's story

Kelly was eleven when she got meningitis. Climbing into bed one evening after soccer practice, there was nothing to show that a serious infection was brewing.

Kelly developed a fever in the night, and her arm hurt. In the morning, her parents took her to see the family doctor. He arranged an X-ray of her arm at the local hospital.
When she undressed for the X-ray, the technician noticed black and blue blotches all over her body. Kelly remembers: 'He got a scared look on his face.'

Kelly was immediately admitted to hospital, where she rapidly took a turn for the worse. She was flown to the nearest children's hospital, with her parents following on by car.

In intensive care

Doctors in the **Intensive Care Unit** warned Kelly's parents that she was very sick and might even die. Her mum says, 'There were tubes everywhere going into and out of her body and there were monitors and machines beeping all around. She looked so small and helpless. All we could do was watch and pray while the doctors treated her.'

Finally, after fighting for her life for a week, Kelly started to improve. She was allowed to move to a normal hospital room. It was only then that her parents found out the name of the terrible illness that had almost killed their child – meningococcal disease.

Having meningitis can mean a long stay in hospital.

Terrible after-effects

Although she was now out of danger, Kelly still had many serious problems to face and she wasn't able to go back to school for the rest of the year. The disease had damaged much of her skin, leaving painful wounds that took months to heal. One was so bad that her brother said it looked like a shark bite! Her doctors were afraid that she might never be able to walk properly again.

Kelly had many weeks of special treatment in hospital, including surgery to graft new skin on to her wounds. Finally, she was able to go home again. Now, several years on, Kelly still has some problems but things are improving. Her walking is back to normal – she can even run – and she is doing very well at school. Of her illness she says, 'This is such a nasty disease that I am praying there might be a cure some day.'

Meningococcal septicaemia can cause severe damage to the skin.

Antibiotic treatment

Antibiotics are medicines that kill or slow down the growth of **bacteria**, but not **viruses**. Antibiotics are the main type of treatment for bacterial meningitis.

There are many different kinds of antibiotics. Each is effective against a particular range of bacteria. Doctors prescribe antibiotics every day to help fight off common illnesses such as throat and ear infections. When it comes to bacterial meningitis and **septicaemia**, treating them as quickly as possible with the right antibiotic can save lives.

How are they given?

Antibiotics are usually given as tablets or liquid to swallow. However, this is quite a slow way of getting the medicine into the bloodstream. Antibiotics for meningitis are given **intravenously** – by injection into a vein – which means that they can immediately circulate around the bloodstream to reach the brain and **meninges**. The antibiotic most likely to be used in meningitis is penicillin. If the patient is allergic to it, another antibiotic will be used.

Early treatment

When someone has bacterial meningitis, he or she needs antibiotics as soon as possible. With most other infections, the doctor or nurse will take samples, such as blood, urine, faeces or a swab of a wound, before giving antibiotics. This is so that the bacteria can be grown and identified from the sample before they are killed by the antibiotic.

If **meningococcal disease** is suspected, there may be no time for taking samples. The doctor will probably give an injection of an antibiotic immediately, before admission to hospital. This makes it harder for the laboratory to grow bacteria from any samples that are later taken from the patient (see page 33). In this case, that is not the most important thing.

Preventing meningitis

Giving a medicine to a healthy person to prevent him or her from getting a disease is called chemoprophylaxis. If someone is diagnosed with **meningococcal meningitis**, then an antibiotic, usually Rifampicin, is given as chemoprophylaxis to their close contacts, such as family members and any boyfriends or girlfriends. This is to prevent further spread of the bacteria and more cases occurring. If there are a number of connected cases of meningococcal meningitis, then antibiotics may be given to other contacts, such as those in the same school or day nursery.

Antibiotics, such as Rifampicin (shown here) may be given to close contacts of people with meningococcal meningitis.

Vaccination

There is no **vaccine** that protects against all forms of meningitis. Good vaccines are available for some forms of bacterial meningitis. For example, there is a safe and effective vaccine against **Hib meningitis** (see pages 20–21). Hib meningitis is now very rare in the countries that use the vaccine. Yet there are some important types of meningitis for which there is still no vaccine.

Military recruits in the USA are vaccinated against various diseases, including meningitis. Today, safety gloves are always worn by medical staff.

Meningococcal vaccines

There is no one single vaccine that will protect against all of the groups of **meningococcus** (A, B, C, Y and W-135). A vaccine that protects against groups A, C, Y and W-135 may be given to those travelling to countries with a high rate of meningitis. This is the vaccine that Muslims have before they go on the Hajj to Saudi Arabia (see page 29). In the USA, this vaccine is offered to new college students and is given to all military recruits.

A new meningococcus group C vaccine has been introduced in the last few years for children and young people in the UK and has proved very effective. Australia also now uses this vaccine routinely for children. But there is no effective vaccine for group B meningitis, which is the most common form in the UK and occurs frequently in many other countries. Trials of a new vaccine in New Zealand look promising.

Pneumococcal vaccines

There are two types of vaccine that can be used to protect against **pneumococcal meningitis**. The first, an older vaccine, is effective but does not work in infants under two years old. A second vaccine has now been developed that is effective in this young age group.

In most **developed countries**, these vaccines are used for people who are at high risk of getting pneumococcal disease (see page 18). In Australia, babies from Aboriginal families, who are at an especially high risk of pneumococcal disease, are vaccinated. In the USA, all parents are now offered the new vaccine for their babies.

The developing world

Giving vaccines would make a huge difference to people in **developing countries**, especially those in Africa where many die in **epidemics** of **meningococcal meningitis**. However, many of these countries cannot afford enough vaccines. International aid organizations are trying to persuade the richer countries to help their poorer neighbours by making these life-saving vaccines more affordable.

Controlling an outbreak

Over the years, there have been many **outbreaks** of **meningococcal meningitis** in schools and colleges. These usually lead to a great deal of coverage in the media. Sometimes, sensational stories can cause worry and even panic within the local community. In most **developed countries**, outbreaks of meningitis are dealt with quickly and efficiently by teams of experts in infection control.

These school children are being vaccinated during a meningitis outbreak in Cheshire, UK.

An outbreak in Wales

An outbreak happened in the Pontypridd area of South Wales in the UK, in early 1999. It started when a fifteen-year-old boy from a local high school contracted meningococcal meningitis and, unfortunately, died. Because it seemed to be one isolated case, the Public Health Department followed the rules for this situation and just gave **antibiotics** to his close family contacts.

Later that week, several more pupils from the same school developed meningitis. Others in the surrounding community also became ill, and one teacher from a neighbouring school died. It was clear that this was a true outbreak and further steps had to be urgently taken.

An Outbreak Control Team was set up. This was a committee that included representatives from the public health department, the local hospital and the local schools. The team made the decision to give antibiotics to every pupil in the school – all 1000 of them! The antibiotics were given out at the school on a Sunday, with healthcare staff working late into the evening so that everyone could be seen.

By the time the outbreak was over, there had been thirteen cases in total, and three people had died.

The media

Any disease that can lead to sudden deaths among children will cause fear and anxiety. Newspaper and television reports often add to this anxiety by deliberately using sensational language such as 'killer bugs' or 'deadly disease' and exaggerating the risks involved.

But when the media get it right, they can have a very important role to play in educating the public about diseases like meningitis. One of the aims of the many voluntary meningitis organizations is to provide journalists with the true facts about this condition so that their stories will inform, not scare, their readers.

How can modern science help?

Meningitis has been the focus of a great deal of research in recent years. Most attention has been directed to three areas: **vaccines**, **diagnostic tests** and genetics.

New vaccines

Vaccination is the only way to prevent meningitis. However, there is one type of **meningococcus**, Group B, for which there is no vaccine. This is a big problem because Group B meningococci cause most cases of meningitis in many **developed countries**. Scientists are working on the development of an effective Group B vaccine, and in some areas, trials of suitable vaccines will be starting soon.

Interestingly, there is one country in the world that does have an effective vaccine against their type of Group B meningococci – Cuba. Unfortunately, the Cuban vaccine does not work well in other countries. It does not protect against the types of this **micro-organism** found elsewhere.

Diagnosis

People with suspected meningitis are often given **antibiotics** before they reach hospital. In this case, it can then be difficult to find live **bacteria** in their blood and **cerebrospinal fluid** samples because the antibiotics have already killed them. More sophisticated tests are needed, which do not depend upon the presence of live bacteria. There is also a need for tests that give rapid results to help doctors to make quick decisions about treatment.

There are already some rapid diagnostic tests for meningitis. A lot of research is being carried out to make them better and more effective. In the future, it may be possible to discover which bacteria is causing the disease from a simple blood test.

Genetic research

In recent years, a lot of hard work has been done by scientists to map out the genetic material – the genome – of some of the important bacteria that cause meningitis. Researchers believe that they have found the complete sequence of genes of meningococci Group A (which cause epidemics in some developing countries) and Group B.

Understanding the genetic make-up of these bacteria should help scientists to understand exactly how the disease can be combatted. In turn, this knowledge should help in the production of new vaccines and perhaps new cures.

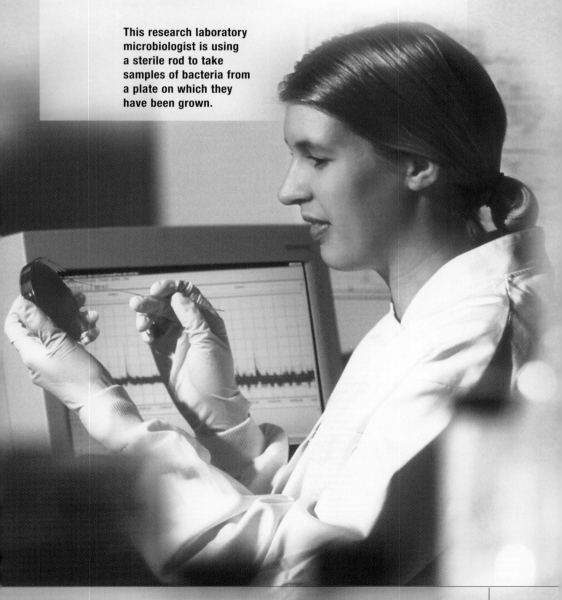

This research laboratory microbiologist is using a sterile rod to take samples of bacteria from a plate on which they have been grown.

Meningitis in the future

In these days of **antibiotics** and vaccinations, it is easy to believe that infectious diseases no longer have the same destructive power that they had in the past. Meningitis, and in particular **meningococcal meningitis**, shows how false that impression can be.

Every year, even in countries with excellent healthcare, people die from meningitis and many more are left with disabling after-effects. It is important that this disease is taken seriously – that people learn about the symptoms and how important it is to seek immediate medical help.

The situation is improving. New vaccinations have made some forms of meningitis almost a thing of the past in some countries. Many children are now alive and well because they had protection against a disease that might otherwise have had severe consequences. And there are real grounds for hoping that this success will continue as new **vaccines** become available.

"Our vision is a world free from meningitis and septicaemia."

(The Meningitis Research Foundation, UK)

Increasing awareness

For the individual, the most effective way to prevent the severe consequences of meningitis is to seek medical help as soon as possible. This means it is vital that people know more about meningitis so that they can recognize the symptoms. This is one of the main roles of charitable organizations like the National Meningitis Association in the USA, the Meningitis Research Foundation in the UK, the Meningitis Centre in Australia and others.

These organizations exist to tell people about meningitis – its causes, symptoms and treatment. They encourage and support further research into this disease. Many of them were set up by survivors of meningitis and their families. Their experiences affected them so deeply that they wanted to educate as many people as possible about meningitis. As Kelly (see page 40) says, 'I try to tell as many people as possible how nasty this disease is and what its symptoms are so maybe I can save someone some day.'

Information and advice

Many organizations offer information and advice on meningitis. They provide information for the media, and encourage and fund research. These groups were often set up by parents and others who had been affected by meningitis.

Contacts in the USA

Meningitis Foundation of America
The Meningitis Foundation of America Inc., 6610 North Shadeland Avenue, Suite 200, Indianapolis, Indiana 46220-4393
Tel: (800) 668-1129
Outside North America: (317) 595-6383
Administrative line: (317) 595-6384 ext 281
Fax: (317) 595-6370
Website: www.musa.org
The Foundation offers information about meningitis as well as support for those affected. The website contains many true-life stories of people who have survived meningitis as well as those who were not so fortunate.

National Meningitis Association
22910 Chestnut Road
Lexington Park, MD 20653
Tel: 1-866-FONE-NMA or 1 866 366-3662
Fax: 1 770 973-7592
Email: support@nmaus.org
Website: www.nmaus.org
The National Meningitis Association offers information about meningitis with a special emphasis on encouraging parents to have their children vaccinated.

Contacts in the UK

Meningitis Research Foundation
Head Office, Midland Way
Thornbury, Bristol, BS35 2BS
Tel: 01454 281811
24-hour helpline: freefone 080 8800 3344
Fax: 01454 281094
Website: www.meningitis.org
The first priority of the Meningitis Research Foundation is research into meningitis. It has a 24-hour helpline providing up-to-date information about meningitis to both the general public and the media, as well as supporting those affected by meningitis through a network of befrienders.

Meningitis Trust
Head Office, Fern House, Bath Road
Stroud, Gloucestershire, GL5 3TJ
Tel: 01453 768000
Fax: 01453 768001
24-hour nurse-led helpline: 0845 6000 800
Email: info@meningitis-trust.org
Website: www.meningitis-trust.org
Schools website:
www.meningitis-learning.org
Health professionals' website:
www.inmedonline.com
The Meningitis Trust is an internationally respected charity with a strong community focus. It has three main aims: to provide support for people affected by meningitis, to educate both the public and health professionals about meningitis, and to fund life-saving research.

Contacts in New Zealand

National Meningitis Trust of New Zealand
PO Box 33-680, Takapuna
Tel: (021) 491 008
Website: www.meningitis.org.nz
The National Meningitis Trust of New Zealand, formerly known as the NZ Meningitis Foundation, offers support to those who have been affected by meningitis. It also produces a range of fact sheets on the condition.

Meningitis Trust
New Zealand Office, PO Box 755
Whangaparaoa, Hibiscus Coast 1463
Tel: (64) 09 428 0828
24-hour free-call nurse-led helpline:
Tel: 0800 446 087
Fax: (64) 09 428 0128
Email: info@meningitis-trust.org.nz
Website: www.meningitis-trust.org.nz

Contacts in Australia

The Meningitis Centre
Telethon Institute for Child Health Research
100 Roberts Road, Subiaco, WA 6008
Or:
PO Box 855, West Perth, WA 6872
Tel: (08) 9489 7791
Fax: (08) 9489 7705
(Hours 9 a.m.–5.00 p.m. WST)
Free call helpline: 1800 250 223
Website: www.meningitis.com.au
The Meningitis Centre provides information about meningitis and offers support to those affected by this condition via a telephone helpline and face-to-face counselling.

Meningitis Foundation
Australian Office
Level 1, Bridgepoint, 3 Brady Street, Mosman, NSW 2088 or:
PO Box 654, Spit Junction,
NSW 2088
Tel: (02) 9960 0051
24-hour free call helpline: 1800 129 068
Fax: (02) 9960 0050
Website:
www.meningitis-trust.org/area/australia.php

Further Reading

Feather: A Child's Life and Death, by Robert Peters; University of Wisconsin Press, 1997.
A father recalls the brief life and sudden death of his four-year-old son, Feather.

Meningitis (Diseases and People), by Edward Willett; Enslow publishers, 1999.
This book is currently out of print but may be available in the library.

Disclaimer
All the Internet addresses (URLs) given in this book were valid at the time of going to press. However, due to the dynamic nature of the Internet, some addresses may have changed, or sites may have changed or ceased to exist since publication. While the author and Publisher regret any inconvenience this may cause readers, no responsibility for any such changes can be accepted by either the author or the Publisher.

Glossary

amputation
removing a part or all of a limb (arm, leg, finger, toe) during surgery

antibiotics
medicines that kill bacteria

antibodies
protein molecules that are made by the defence cells of the body to fight off harmful organisms

arthritis
soreness and swelling of the joints

bacteria
tiny living organisms, some of which cause disease

cerebrospinal fluid (CSF)
the clear, watery fluid that bathes the brain and spinal cord

colonization
when bacteria live harmlessly in or on another living organism, such as the human body

developed countries
a term used to describe those countries with many industries, a complex economic system and a generally high standard of living – such as those in Western Europe and the USA

developing countries
a term used to describe poorer countries, such as those in Sub-Saharan Africa, that are trying to make their industry and economic system more advanced

diagnostic tests
methods used by healthcare staff to find out which disease a patient has

epidemic
an outbreak of a disease in which large numbers of people are affected; if a disease is said to be epidemic, this means that it usually goes away between outbreaks

epilepsy
a serious medical condition which makes a person have seizures – brief periods of time during which they lose control of their bodies due to abnormal electrical activity in the brain

fungi
plant-like organisms that may sometimes cause human disease

Hib meningitis
a type of bacterial meningitis that particularly affects young children

HIV (Human Immunodeficiency Virus) infection
the viral infection that leads to the condition known as AIDS

immune system
the cells and organs of the body that help it to defend itself from attack by harmful organisms

inflammation
a condition in which a body part becomes red, sore and swollen

Intensive Care Unit (ICU)
part of a hospital where very ill patients are looked after by specially trained staff

intravenously
by injection directly into a vein

lumbar puncture
diagnostic test for meningitis – a fine needle is used to take a sample of cerebrospinal fluid; the lumbar region is the area of the lower back where the needle is inserted

membrane
thin layer of tissue that covers parts inside the body

meninges
the three fine membranes that surround and protect the brain and spinal cord

meningococcal disease
a term used to describe infection with the meningococcal bacteria, causing meningitis and/or septicaemia

meningococcal meningitis
one of the main types of bacterial meningitis, a life-threatening infection that can be treated with antibiotics

meningococcus
a common way of referring to the bacterium *Neisseria meningitidis*, which causes a serious form of meningitis

microbiology laboratory
the place where samples are examined to see if they are infected with bacteria

micro-organisms
tiny living things that may cause disease – viruses and bacteria are micro-organisms

outbreak
an outbreak of meningitis is said to occur when two or more people in a group (such as a school) or a small geographical area get meningitis caused by the same organism

photophobia
abnormal sensitivity to bright lights

pneumococcal meningitis
one of the main types of bacterial meningitis, a life-threatening infection that can be treated with antibiotics

pneumonia
a serious infection of the lungs that can be caused by pneumococcal bacteria

protozoa
tiny, single-celled creatures that may sometimes cause disease

sanitation
safe disposal of human bodily waste and provision of a clean water supply

septicaemia
a serious bacterial infection of the blood, also known as blood poisoning

serogroups
slightly different forms of the same bacteria

sickle cell disorder
a blood disorder that means that some red blood cells are an abnormal shape

spinal cord
the thick bundle of nerve tissue that lies inside the bones of the spine

spleen
an organ that lies just under the ribs on the left hand side of the body and forms part of the immune system

sub-Saharan Africa
the African countries that lie south of the Sahara desert; the poorer countries in Africa generally lie in this area

tissues
the mass of cells that form the different parts of the body

tuberculosis
a bacterial disease that usually affects the lungs but may also sometimes cause meningitis

vaccine
a substance that is given, usually by injection, to healthy people in order to prevent them from catching a particular infectious disease in the future

viruses
tiny organisms that are just like bags of chemicals, many of which cause disease

white blood cells
cells of the immune system that circulate in the blood ready to defend the body against attack

Index

Titles in the *Need to Know* series include:

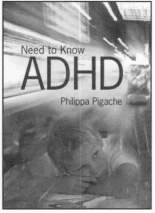

Need to Know
ADHD
Philippa Pigache

Hardback   0 431 18840 8

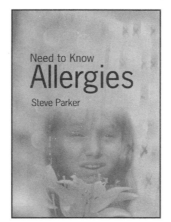

Need to Know
Allergies
Steve Parker

Hardback   0 431 09760 7

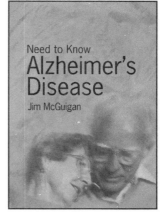

Need to Know
Alzheimer's Disease
Jim McGuigan

Hardback   0 431 18841 6

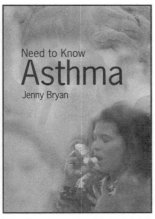

Need to Know
Asthma
Jenny Bryan

Hardback   0 431 09761 5

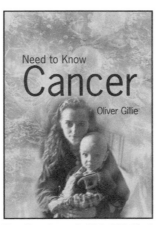

Need to Know
Cancer
Oliver Gillie

Hardback   0 431 18842 4

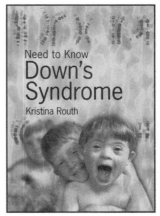

Need to Know
Down's Syndrome
Kristina Routh

Hardback   0 431 18843 2

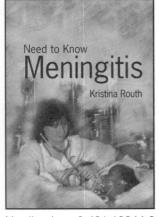

Need to Know
Meningitis
Kristina Routh

Hardback   0 431 18844 0

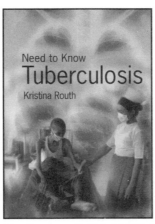

Need to Know
Tuberculosis
Kristina Routh

Hardback   0 431 18845 9

Find out about the other titles in this series on our website www.heinemann.co.uk/library